SIT YOUR BLACK A.S.S. DOWN!

A Parent's Guide to Preventing
African-American Boys from Becoming
ANOTHER SOCIAL STATISTIC
in Public Schools

Miranda Y. Pearson

Miranda Y. Pearson
P.O. Box 1108
Benson, NC 27504
(919)894-8002
divineapptcounseling@yahoo.com
www.divineapptcounseling.com

Limits of Liability and Disclaimer of Warranty

The author and publisher shall not be liable for your misuse of this material. This book is strictly for informational and educational purposes.

Warning – Disclaimer

The purpose of this book is to educate and inform. The author and publisher do not guarantee that anyone following these techniques, suggestions, tips, ideas, or strategies will become successful. The author and publisher shall have neither liability nor responsibility to anyone with respect to any loss or damage caused, or alleged to be caused, directly or indirectly by the information contained in this book.

ISBN   978-1-941749-49-4

Printed in the United States of America

Chattanooga, TN 37411

Dedication

This book is dedicated to every African-American male whose purpose and destiny is great, despite what statistics say about you.

To every parent of an African-American male, who have become frustrated with public school. Hold on; help is on the way!

To every public school employee, teacher, administrator who loves other people's children, despite statistics. **THANK YOU!!!**

To all of my former students who made me a lover of all students. You have been, by far, the best "job" I've ever had the pleasure of working.

To my husband, Robert, who has always been my number one supporter and friend. You have believed in me at times when I stopped believing in myself. **I love you!**

And finally, to my son, Joshua, who will forever be my greatest, most treasured "assignment". The African-American male who changed my life forever. You have taught me the true meaning of unconditional love, and I love you to the moon and back. Beyond infinity. As long as live, I will fight hard **not** to allow you, or anyone else's son, to become ANOTHER SOCIAL STATISTIC!

Contents

Introduction...vii

"Who is the A. S. S.?" 11

"I Had to Move My Clip to Red!" 19

"What Does Learning Look Like?"............................. 27

"My Teacher Doesn't Like Me!"................................. 37

"You Are the Lead Teacher!"...................................... 45

"What Now?" 49

Introduction

As I sat and listened to the second-grade teachers tell us, the parents, about their various classrooms, educational and behavioral expectations of our children, their students, I cringed within. Most of their "presentation" consisted of new curriculum additions, what to do with daily folders (as they came home), and how students would be consistently tested throughout the academic year. I smiled as the teacher intern talked about the "one" lone field trip students "might" be able to participate contingent upon their behavior and the results of their constant testing. I wondered as they all spoke, one by one, "...with all of this testing "work," who would have the time to get to know a student, or heaven forbid, to indulge in a little bit of classroom fun?" Not one teacher spoke of how their love for teaching and their love of children would be their number one priority, or how they would make sure our students would be their very best, based on their abilities and interests and not just behavior reports and test results.

Echoing in my mind was the conversation I recently had with my son, about his "intense dislike" for school. He said, "Mom, please don't make me go back! I hate school!" "Why?", I asked. "Because" he said, "it's boring and all we do is work!" Now, to an educator (this marked my nineteenth year in education, ranging from a classroom teacher, guidance counselor, assistant principal intern, to a district-wide administrator), this was incredibly disappointing and sad. But as a mom, I became extremely protective, as well as frightened, because as a child, I loved school! As a child, school was exciting, yet challenging. School was a place of discipline, yet nurturing. I fell in love with education and learning simultaneously. It was a teacher, Ms. Audrey Justice, from Roanoke, Virginia, who made me fall in love with teaching. Ms. Justice was eclectic, smart, wisecracking and loving. She wore Birkenstocks, thick socks, short hair and smelled of cigarettes, but you could never be wrong or an undisciplined student in Audrey Justice's class. You were always a scholar, and she made everyone feel important to her, as well as to the world. As I thought about my child hating school, I wondered, "would his teacher be an Audrey Justice and love his purpose out of him or would she perpetuate his disdain for school forever?"

As a public school employee, I knew that my son's hatred of school was somewhat justified. In a Millennial society, the Dewey Decimal system of conducting school is antiquated, boring, and more test results driven, than relationship focused.

As my son begs me not to take him to school, I say a silent prayer that God would enlighten his teacher to see him, not as **A**nother **S**ocial **S**tatistic, not as an at-risk student because he's talkative and likes to wiggle in his seat. I prayed she would see him as a bright, energetic seven-year-old, who loves football, basketball, video games, bugs, and his dog Oreo. I hope she sees my son, born with purpose, born with destiny. As his teacher, I hope that she recognizes her assignment is to discover and to nurture this purpose.

I created this guide for all parents who love their sons. I am writing to those who have become frustrated because their sons are frustrated and to those who need guidance in navigating the public school system to ensure it will not fail their child – not just academically but socially and emotionally as well. This guide is intended to empower you as a parent! It will aid you on how NOT to allow society or public school to label your son as...

ANOTHER SOCIAL STATISTIC!

1

"Who is the A. S. S.?"

"Everybody is a genius. But if you judge a fish on its ability to climb a tree, it will live its whole life believing that it is stupid."
Albert Einstein

N ow that I have your attention with the title of my book, let me begin by saying that by no means is this book going to "bash" public education or public school teachers, administrators, or support personnel. I am not an angry or disgruntled ex-school employee or parent. However, I **AM** passionate about all children, in particular, children of color, more specifically, African-American boys, because, after a career in public education, I have seen them left behind on purpose! While I don't believe it began as intentional, it has become a major problem and from an educator's, as well as a parent's point-of-view, I want to share wisdom to aid you in navigating public school for your son's success.

The title of the book stems from one of my many visits into a public school to analyze a "problem" student. My assignment was to observe the student to assess non-compliant, non-conforming or otherwise obstinate behavior toward the teacher and other classmates. However, as I observed the student, I also observed the teacher's interactions with the student, the teacher's reaction to the "problem" student, as well as the atmosphere the teacher set for this "problem" student, and the other students within the classroom. More times than I can count, the "problem" student would be a child of color, more specifically an African American male. Most of the "problem" students of color had the same characteristics: male, inattentive, physically active, socially friendly, resistant to authority, little to no parental involvement, and what was most noticeable, this student was academically behind his peers in all subjects, especially language arts/reading.

What prompted me in writing this chapter was a visit to a third-grade classroom, I made many years ago, to observe Maurice (the name has been changed to protect the identity of the student) whose teacher complained that he "...just won't do anything at all, and he disturbs other students around him so that they are unable to learn and focus." In addition to her complaint of not doing anything within the classroom, she stated that she believed that Maurice was a bully.

When I entered the classroom Maurice was indeed "socializing" with another student, but so were all of the other students within the class. I took a seat at the back of the classroom and of course, there were a few students who noticed my presence and said "Hello" or asked each other, "Who is that lady?" I smiled politely and nodded my head because the teacher was telling them all to find their seats and sit down. I noticed there were a few African-American students within the class, (Maurice was the only African-American male) and there was a hearing impaired student as well. The teacher began her lesson on the smart board and eventually asked questions of the class. Maurice was seated on the front row, directly in front of the teacher. She asked questions and called on the same three students the entire hour I was in the class. Every time the teacher asked a question, Maurice raised his hand, and there were times he chanted, "me, me, I know the answer." There were other times when he stood abruptly out of his chair to ensure that she saw his hand was up. She neither spoke to him directly nor acknowledged he was even in the room, except to glare at him. Eventually, Maurice began to talk with the student beside him, and he ended up rolling around on the floor. At this point, what do you think the teacher did? Right! You guessed it! "Maurice, your behavior is out of hand! Go to the Principal's office right now!", she said. Now, what do you think was Maurice's reaction? I can imagine, judging by his facial expressions and the slump of his shoulders, shame, embarrassment, and his reputation, "since you tried to "play me" in front of my friends," I can imagine Maurice saying to himself, "I'm not going to go quietly and willingly." The interaction between the teacher and Maurice became confrontational, and I ended up intervening by volunteering to walk Maurice to the Principal's office. As we were leaving the classroom, Maurice was mumbling loudly about how "he didn't care, and he didn't like her or her class anyway." Once outside of the classroom, I asked Maurice to calm down, take a deep breath and tell me what happened. (Remember there are always three sides to every story, his side, her side, and the truth).

Maurice said, "Man that lady hates me! She always gets me into trouble! I hate her class, and I hate her! I wasn't doing anything to her, yet she always makes me go to the office and then I get in trouble!" Now, remember I said there is his side (interpretation), her side (interpretation) and the truth (what actually happened). From Maurice's vantage point, his teacher did not like him and from his teacher's vantage point, Maurice was a troublemaker. Well, having been the person to witness "the truth", there was some validity from both of their vantage points and neither exhibited behavior that would rectify the situation, but their behavior exacerbated the situation.

I informed the Principal of what I witnessed within the classroom. "Yes, Maurice is very busy, active, and can be a distraction to his classmates, however, his teacher totally dismisses him, despite his good, calm, and engaged behavior and the daggered looks were menacing.", I said. (By the way, it was Maurice's teacher's facial expressions that birthed the title of my book, in addition to the conversations that I have heard in teacher's lounges and faculty meetings. "No" she never asked Maurice to "...sit his black A- - down", but her disapproving glare, toward him, said that and a lot more).

A Question to Ponder

Based on the above scenario, exactly, who is the A.S.S.? (**A**nother **S**ocial **S**tatistic). Is Maurice an A.S.S. because he can't behave in his teacher's classroom or is his teacher an A.S.S. because she has never taken the time to know Maurice as a person or find out how best to maximize his learning potential in her class?

What is my parental advice for you? Don't leave your son in a classroom where he is not successful and you never find out why. You need to establish clear and consistent communication before he ever enters a classroom. You have to know that it is perfectly okay and legal for you to "interview" your child's teacher based on your child's abilities, personality, proclivities, and life's purpose.

A.S.S. Prevention Steps

☐ Find out what your child's teacher's philosophy of teaching consist of. Does she/he believe ALL students can learn?

☐ Does she/he love other people's children?

☐ Is teaching just a job to provide financial assistance or is it a lifelong dream, goal or passion?

☐ Ask about all teaching experiences. In particular, is she/he culturally competent to teach your child?

☐ Ask about her teaching style and classroom management techniques.

☐ Be honest about your child's behavior(s), attitude toward school, former relationships with educators and previous grades. It is better to have this conversation yourself, rather than the teacher discuss your son's difficulties with a former teacher and form an "opinion" based on someone else's experience with your child.

Your interview/conversation with the teacher will let them know, up front, that you are willing and able to be an informed and involved parent who will team with them to ensure the best possible academic school year for your child.

If for any reason during the interview you are not at ease with the conversation or the teacher's answers, then it is your right to request a conference with the building administrator to discuss your concerns. If it is well into the school year and your child is unsuccessful, then you need to request an immediate conference with both the teacher and the principal. Don't allow the principal to dismiss you and your concerns. If you are not satisfied with your outcomes there, then take your concerns to the Superintendent's office. Please **DOCUMENT EVERYTHING** discussed in all meetings. If you do not document your discussions, save emails or voice mails, then they simply did not occur.

Oh, I almost forgot to tell you about the outcome in regards to Maurice. I explained to the Principal (without Maurice being in the room) my concerns about how the teacher ignored him (bad attention, to a child, is better than no attention) and only called on the same three students. I also informed the Principal that the teacher's entire classroom was out of their seats and talking very loudly upon my entering the room, not just Maurice. (It was only after I sat down, the teacher began a group lesson in which the students sat and paid attention to the lesson). The teacher not only ignored Maurice, but she was insensitive to the hearing impaired student, at one point replying to him, "Did you not hear what I said to you?" (This student was wearing two rather large hearing aids and a few kids snickered from her remarks). She never smiled the entire time I was in the classroom, even to the students she called upon, and they gave correct answers. Her response was neither "good job" nor "way to go", she just quickly moved on to another question.

"In all honesty," I said to the Principal, "Maurice is not this teacher's only problem, he is just her scapegoat." The principal did not look shocked or upset at my comment, but only nodded her head in agreement as if to say, "I know." Maurice was allowed to go into another classroom for the remainder of the day and, after some gentle prodding from Central Services, was switched to another teacher, where he completed a successful academic year in 3rd grade.

Parent's Tip: Don't let your student become an **A.S.S.** (Another Social Statistic) on your watch!

2

"I Had to Move My Clip to Red!"

"An effective teacher manages a classroom. An ineffective teacher disciplines a classroom."
Harry Wong

Behavior is a major concern within public schools. In the wake of multiple shootings, schools have become cautious and have adopted a zero tolerance level on weapons, fighting, gangs, bullying, harassment, discrimination, and intimidation. Targeted focus or skill development is expected to increase upon assessment. "Bell- to-bell" instruction is required, and a greater emphasis is placed upon teachers to have students in lower grade levels, to be ready for third-grade testing. This elevated priority leaves little to no room for students to socialize or to be active, particularly in the elementary level. It takes a special teacher to possess the ability to teach each child individually, according to their academic level, as well as maintain a healthy balance between socialization, physical activity, and instruction.

Allow me to introduce you to Louis. Louis was the class clown. In "trouble" since preschool, Louis had no interest in school at all. Initially, he attended to socialize, but his preschool teacher complained to his mother, every day, about his "disruptive behavior."

"Louis doesn't lay down when it's time to take a nap."

"Louis talks during lunchtime."

"Louis takes his shoes off in the classroom while the teacher is teaching."

"Louis doesn't like to share on the playground."

"Louis talks out of turn when the teacher is asking questions."

"Louis wiggles in his seat and can't seem to be still!"

These are just a handful of complaints that Louis's mother received, on a daily basis, from his preschool teacher. Louis's mother began to punish him for his behavior; no T.V., no toys, no computer time and no playing outside when he gets home. It became so severe that Louis was not allowed to do anything extracurricular for about a month. One day, Louis's dad decided to pay the preschool an unannounced visit. He stood outside the door of the classroom and noticed that it was very noisy. He peeked inside, through the window on the door, and saw the students everywhere. As he describes it, "they were climbing the walls." Louis was a number within the bunch, but not the ONLY number who was in "trouble". Louis's father made a note of this and decided that he would not confront the teacher yet, but would wait a few more days and come back for another unannounced visit.

When he returned, he came during naptime; he heard the teacher say, "Good job Haylie!" "Way to go Joey!" "Sweet dreams Julio!" and when she got to Louis she said, "Dream about butterflies and baseballs Louis!" who promptly said, "I caught a butterfly yesterday with my mom!" The teacher told Louis to be quiet, but he wanted to talk about the butterflies and baseballs that she told him to dream about. At this point, Louis's dad opened the door, went inside and told the teacher that he had come to pick Louis up early, and he and Louis left together. Louis's dad took him to get ice cream and apologized for punishing him, daily, for his behavior. Louis's dad realized that at age four Louis was acting and conducting himself age appropriately. He also realized that the problem within Louis's classroom wasn't behavioral issues, but a classroom management issue. Not only was it a classroom management issue, but the preschool is supposed to aid in "child development." How would a four year- old know how to handle their behavior without being taught. Isn't that the purpose of school?

Louis's father went home and talked to his wife about his discoveries, first of the classroom management issues on the previous visit and finally on the teacher demanding quiet during naptime, as she is going around the room talking loudly to each student. Although no other student spoke to her but Louis, his father still viewed it as her engaging him in conversation and not the other way around.

Both Louis's parents realized they had allowed the school to be more concerned about Louis's behavior than they were about what he was learning academically. They were disappointed that school seemed to want toy soldiers, who sat up straight in the chair, while looking straight ahead, with no character or conversation. They desired a place where Louis could discover, not only who he was becoming, but a love of learning.

Yes, behavior is important! Learning how to navigate with a good attitude and social skills is a very necessary skill in today's society. Learning is more than behavior clips, behavior charts, and "what color am I on?"

In my household, our lives, at one point, had become consumed with what color my son was on, not knowing that this tiny little smiley face, colored to indicate his daily behavior in class, was causing him anxiety, stress and an eventual hatred toward going to school. (A purple smiley face was excellent, a blue smiley face was great, a green smiley face was good, a yellow smiley face was a warning, and a red smiley face was not good at all). "What's the point of going to school mom? he said. "The minute I get there, my teacher is going to tell me to move my clip to red, and I'll be in trouble for the remainder of the day!"

Wow! How sobering to realize that he already felt defeated before the class even started. You see, just like Louis and Maurice, my son was a talker (so was his mama) and he often became inattentive and, therefore, began to fidget. This behavior almost always warranted him an opportunity to move his clip to red, and unless he was extremely quiet and still for the remainder of the day, red is more than likely his "resting spot."

It is easy to internalize your child's behavior and take it personally. Although society sees behavior as a reflection of parenting, it appears to be more harshly judged in the African-American male student's life. African-American boys are more likely than their Caucasian counterparts, to be sent to timeout, another classroom to "chill out", or as a request from the teacher, be removed out of the classroom because of their behavior. In 2008, Pedro A. Noguera wrote a book detailing the problems with African-American boys in public education, and in 2016, those issues still prevail. Pedro A. Noguera believes that public schools, in the United States, are not alarmed that they have failed African-American boys. He surmises that black males are underrepresented in academic achievement programs and are over-represented in disciplinary reform programs (Noguera, 2008). The goal of being in school is to learn and learning only takes place when the student is in the classroom, not out of it. As a parent, how can you combat the fear of the dreaded behavior chart?

More A.S.S. Prevention Steps

1) Don't punish your child for a teacher who has poor classroom management skills.

If the teacher tells you in one sentence all of the "unacceptable behaviors" that your son has displayed, but within the next sentence she says, "but he is not the only one", then it's not a matter of your son being unruly or bad, but perhaps the teacher has a difficult time managing all of the behaviors in the classroom, and your son is one of many. Talk to the Principal about the possibility of moving your son to a more "seasoned" classroom teacher's classroom, where the focus is on learning and not behavior.

2) Don't allow detention, suspension, or expulsion to be the only means of handling what the school calls unacceptable behavior.

Find out what the definition of unacceptable behavior is and set up a conference with your child's teacher to discuss your son's particular behavior(s). If the behaviors are age appropriate, then partner with your son's teacher to maximize his learning experiences without highlighting the unacceptable behavior.

3) Discuss times of day "triggers".

For example, does the unacceptable behavior take place during transitions? Does it happen when your son participates in group work? Does it happen when he doesn't understand the assignment or the instructions? Does it take place after lunch? Ask the teacher to keep a running tally of triggers for about a week, so that you will have a better understanding and can redirect accordingly. It may be something as simple as trading the Kool-Aid pouch at lunch for a box of apple juice instead.

4) Discuss the possibility of making a behavior contract with your son's teacher.

Ascertain what classroom activities your son likes and build the "likes" into the behavior contract. For example, if he loves computer time, then for 30 minutes of computer time he has to have been unacceptable-behavior free for 4 hours during the school day. (You may want to start off with less time if the unacceptable actions are severe). Just like the behavior contract in school, you can also do one for the home.

5) Don't allow your son's teacher to spend an entire academic year doing so much discipline that she is failing to teach.

Sign up to volunteer or be a frequent visitor with lunch or reading time. Usually in elementary school, your presence is not only wanted, it is needed to assist the teacher in any way possible. Keep in mind the teacher is not the enemy. Partner with them to ensure your son receives the best academic support that he can obtain. If his current teacher does not want to partner with you, then request a conference with the principal and politely request another partner.

6) Don't allow your son's behavior to be the springboard for special education classes.

Behavior does not equate to educational deficits, however; it can contribute to it if steps 1-5 are not followed. Public education has been notorious for allowing over identification of African-American students, specifically boys, into the special education arena. Often teachers see it as a way to get rid of their problems and parents aren't often educated in school law and school policies. My advice is to know both! The school's policies should parallel, uphold, and enhance school law. Unfortunately, many Public schools break the law, every day, at the expense of the student's educational welfare and well-being, and often it is because parents are not genuinely educated, informed, and aware as it pertains to their rights.

Parent's Tip: Don't allow teachers, principals, or school officials to intimidate you when it comes to obtaining the best possible education for your child. Don't feel bad or apologize for wanting the best for him.

3

"What Does Learning Look Like?"

"The only thing that interferes with my learning is my education."
Albert Einstein

When I was a classroom teacher; my first year was my worst year! No matter how many classes you take or how many staff developments you participate in, your classroom, your student's attitude toward learning (while they are with you), and your style of teaching are all different.

On my first day on the job, I stood at the door, not smiling as my students filed past me, but scowling as if something smelled rotten. In my mind, I had already rehearsed how this would play out. They would come into the room, one by one and sit down, quietly, and read my instructions on the board, begin to do their seatwork until I checked the roll, and then we would start the lecture. We had 90 minutes for the class (I taught high school English) and all but 10 minutes of that was a lecture. So, after they did their 10- minute seat work activity, I began the lesson on points of plot.

I remember saying, "Please stop talking!"

"Turn around please!"

"Spit that gum out!"

"Sit down!"

"Did you hear what I just said?"

Needless to say, it was a miserable first year! I had spent too much time in the teacher's lounge, and I had prepared myself for the "bad kids" and that is exactly what I received. As well, they received the mean "old teacher" and I was only the ripe 'ole age of 26! You can imagine how I felt when June rolled around! I was relieved and seriously considering going back into the dull world of banking. I loved the idea of teaching, but I went inside my classroom with someone else's classroom management style, lesson plans, and as much as I don't want to admit it, "retired on the job" personality. I had allowed teachers who had lost their zeal for teaching give me "words of wisdom" and advice.

Well, during the break, I had to detoxify myself from all the negative energy that I had stored within and I had to meditate on what a good teacher looked like. I couldn't help but to think about my beloved Audrey Justice, the woman who loved me, despite my incessant talking, and constant wiggling. She was the woman who let me be me, the woman who pulled out likes, dislikes and leadership abilities that I didn't even know that I had. Audrey Justice loved me; she loved all of us, and there wasn't anything that we could do to disappoint her except not learn. We always learned because she kept our attention, we were engaged, and we were always eager and hungry for more. If I go back through my high school class, most of us had Mrs. Justice in 6th grade, and I'm proud to say that out of a graduating class of more than 200, most of us went to college, a few of us have Ph.D.'s, and all of us are successful adults who loved learning.

I knew that after meditating on why learning was so fun for me, I had to change my teaching style, my attitude, and my behavior to accommodate my students.

Fast forward to my second year of teaching, I was smiling at the door, shaking each student by the hand, making eye contact, and saying, "Good morning Mr. So and So" or "Good morning Miss So and So." I made my conversation and eye contact intentional, letting each student know that we are here, together, and we may as well get some learning done. Halogen lamps in every corner, it wasn't the institutionalized overhead lights that loomed out at us, soft jazz wafted through the air as they completed their initial assignment. After a brief 8-10 lecture; and modeling of the classroom assignment, I let them go, to their individual learning stations to complete various assignments that would encompass the remaining 70 minutes of class. After being at each station for roughly 15 minutes, a shifting of the music was the signal to switch. They were allowed to talk, chew gum, eat or drink if I didn't see it, and talk with their peers (every activity called for team collaboration). These were all of the things they desired, and the compromise was that they completed the work and showed competency of each skill learned, for the remaining 10 minutes of class. I no longer had to announce on a daily basis that I was the teacher. They knew that by how I managed their classroom. They were learning, and it was fun.

So, What Does Learning Look Like?

Unfortunately, in public school, some teachers would desire to sift each student through the same "potato grid", but all students are different. Students learn differently and at various paces. The mistake some teachers make is they want the student to adapt to them (they already have a diploma and a degree) instead of adapting to the students to assist them in learning the necessary skills, so they become successful adults.

Let's face it; every student will not go to college, nor will they desire to attend and every student will not aspire to be an entrepreneur. We need to teach every student based on where they are and maintain high levels of expectation.

We must adjust the levels according to their abilities, varying academic levels and more importantly according to their desires.

Five students within a graduating class may aspire to be a doctor, but not all of them necessarily want to be a surgeon. They could be a Doctor of Theology, a Doctor of Philosophy, a Doctor of Medicine, a Doctor of Pharmacology, and a Doctor of Cars (Mechanic). Various forms of what a doctor looks like, but all very successful careers.

Life-long learners are:

➤ Those who are allowed to own their feelings about formal education. Some students learn better in a non-traditional classroom setting, and that is okay! Non-traditional within public education would consist of going outside to write a Haiku (Japanese poetry) instead of staying in the classroom. The outdoors becomes the non-traditional classroom.

➤ Those who learn according to their learning styles. Although there have been conferences and seminars on learning styles and Multiple Intelligences for years, it is rare that a teacher would take the time to inventory each of her students to find out how they learn best.

Learning styles are various ways in which students may prefer to learn information. Their particular learning style allows them to absorb, process, comprehend and retain information. A student's learning style can influence their behavior positively. There are three primary types of learning styles: **visual, kinesthetic, and auditory.**

Visual learners are those students who prefer images to enable them to absorb the learning material. They use images such as maps, charts, or graphic organizers to process and comprehend information. These students use pictures to help them retain what they have learned.

Kinesthetic learners are those students who prefer tactile representation or "hands-on" activities to absorb the learning material. They learn best when the teacher models the lesson and then allows them to demonstrate, in order to process, what was learned. Their finished product allows them to retain the information that they've learned.

Auditory learners are those students who prefer listening and speaking to enable them to absorb the material to be learned. They process information through group work, as well as lectures. They retain by hearing the information and discussing it in depth.

Harvard professor, Howard Gardner, identified Multiple Intelligences. According to his cognitive research, Gardner (1991) was able to distinguish that students were able to absorb, process, comprehend and retain based on various minds, which are individually distinct to accommodate the broad spectrum of students within a school setting. The multiple intelligences, as explained by Dr. Gardner, are **visual-spatial, bodily-kinesthetic, musical, interpersonal, intrapersonal, linguistic, and logical-mathematical.**

Visual –Spatial learners absorb through drawings, verbal, and physical imagery. They would most likely choose a profession that involved space, architecture, or water. They are affected by their environment, and they have a keen sense of discernment. They are intrigued by graphs, charts, models, drawings, videos, and anything multimedia.

Bodily-kinesthetic learners absorb through creating, touching, and moving. Their varied interests are anything dance oriented, acting, role-playing, and things that are tangible and real. They would most likely choose the arts or sciences as a profession.

Musical learners are self-explanatory. They love rhythm; lyrics, speaking, sounds and they are sensitive to their environment. They would most likely choose anything musical, production or acting as a profession.

Interpersonal learners like absorbing through interaction with others through group interactions, writing, conferences, seminars, and email. These students have lots of friends, are empathetic, and street smart. They process information best one on one with the instructor.

Intrapersonal learners are shy, and they would prefer to be independently taught. They like to journal, read, and create and require privacy. They have interests and goals that are not parallel with the crowd, and they gain strength from being intrinsically motivated. They are wise and need little prodding to do well within the academic arena.

Linguistic learners are wordsmiths. They like to read, write poetry, create spoken word and have mastered the art of effective communication. This student has a high interest in all things electronic.

Logical-mathematical learners like to reason; they like to explore; they recognize shapes and patterns that others don't initially see. They like to investigate and play games, form concepts and pay attention to details to solve a problem.

Gardner maintained that if teachers took time (yes it takes time to get to know all of the students individually), they would discover that their methods of teaching would have to vary to accommodate the student, not themselves.

Dear Parents, public education institutions are no longer in the student learning business, but in the political arena business. It's all about politics baby! Schools are being erected based upon property taxes. The nicer the neighborhoods, the better the schools, the more resources, the more PTA/PTO involvement and the more politics rule. Jails, not colleges, are being built based on third-grade test scores. Jails are private, and the people who own them are interested in one thing. Making money. The more prisoners, the more money the state has to pay and the longer they stay, the longer the payment.

Be informed parents! In most states, according to the Schott Foundation for Public Education, it is easier for the public to track the number of incarcerated Black and Latino males, than the number who graduate from high school. About 6% of working age (18-64 years old) African-American men are currently in state or federal prisons or municipal jails. Approximately 34% of all working age African-American men, who are not incarcerated are ex-offenders. April of 2014 PBS reports African-American men falling behind their peers in the classroom. PBS reports only

54% of African-American males graduate from high school, compared to more than 75% of their Caucasian and Asian-American peers.

As a parent and educational professional, I offer the following advice:

Discover your child's primary learning style.

There is a possibility that that there is a struggle with "unacceptable behaviors" because he is bored! It may be that your son is not challenged according to his interests and according to his capacity to learn. Don't wait for the school to give you this information, because they will not. They don't mind testing him for special education classes, and they even would love it if you got him tested with his primary care physician to see if he has ADHD or ADD, but there will be no voluntary testing for learning styles or multiple intelligences. Fortunately for you, there are online tests that you can administer to your son to determine both his learning style and his multiple intelligences.

Request an appointment with the teacher.

Once you find out your son's learning style and multiple intelligence level, make an appointment with his teacher to discuss some ways in which to vary teaching style to accommodate and facilitate his learning. If you are unable to achieve the results from the teacher, then speak with the building administrator. Make sure you have facts, results, and concrete evidence of your subject matter, so they know you are serious and your expectations of them, as well as your son, are high. If you are unable to achieve the level of satisfaction at the school level, then by all means take it to the district. Before going to the superintendent, you may want to talk to the district curriculum facilitator or director (the title is different within each county) and explain what you have learned about your child based on his learning style and multiple intelligence report.

You can find the learning styles test at
www.educationplanner.org
and the multiple intelligences test at
www.edutopia.org/multiple-intelligences-assessment

Parent's Tip: Listen to your son when he says that he hates school or that he is bored with school. His "unacceptable behaviors" may be the result of not being challenged enough in class, not by piling on more work, but by finding out his best style of learning, enhancing the learning experience with his multiple intelligences. Fortunately, we all have varied learning styles and intelligences or else the world would be a very dull place.

4

"My Teacher Doesn't Like Me!"

"The task of the modern educator is not to cut down jungles, but to irrigate deserts."
C.S. Lewis

Having been a classroom teacher, it is tough for me to comprehend that there are those within the classroom who don't care about, let alone love, other people's children. I recall having a teacher, Mrs. Meadow, who was very kind. I don't remember a lot of particular details about her except for the fact that I knew that she cared about me. There was an incident one day when I decided to "make" breasts for myself. You see, I was tiny, very tiny in all areas, and most of my friends, who were girls, were wearing Underoos. Well, I so desperately wanted to be like them, so I went into the girl's bathroom and dampened the hard brown paper towels and stuffed them inside my T-shirt to give me the illusion of having breasts. Well, on this particular day I was the line leader, and Mrs. Meadows gently took me to the side, faced me, with her back to the other students and removed my "breasts". She tossed them in the trash and looked at me, placed her hand on my shoulder and told me not to be so anxious to grow up. She told me that God created me, and he loved me, right now, just the way I am. She gave me a half hug and told me to lead well.

Did you hear what I said? My second-grade teacher, who didn't embarrass me, gave me a quick lesson on God, self-esteem, and timing, then she admonished me to lead well! As I look back over that brief interaction on today, I realize that Mrs. Meadows liked me (she may even have loved me). Although she never told me in those exact words, I know it then, as a seven to eight-year-old, and I know it now because she left a lasting impression upon my soul.

Why did I tell you about Mrs. Meadow? I told you this to let you know that children, no matter how young or old they are, emphatically know whether or not someone likes, loves or tolerates them, even for a minute. It's worth doing a little bit of investigating.

Questions to Ask Your Son

1. What gives you the impression that your teacher does not like you?
2. What does your teacher say to make you feel this way?
3. What is your definition of being liked?
4. How does "being liked" look to you?
5. Is there anyone else in the class who your teacher does not like? How do you know?
6. Is there anyone in the class that your teacher does like? How do you know?
7. What is your favorite thing about school?
8. What do you like most about your class?
9. Do you like your teacher?
10. Name one thing that you know about your teacher. (For example: Is she/he married or does she/he have children?).

After speaking with your child, take a day or two to process what was said. Make sure you take the entire emotionalism aspect out of the conversation and set up an appointment or a conference to meet with your son's teacher to discuss the results of your Q & A session.

Remember, even though the teacher is the educational professional, you need to go in as the professional parent and remember you are a team, both you and the teacher. Your job is to make sure your son has an effective educational journey. Always begin the

conversation by saying you did not come to accuse, but you came because you are concerned that your young son would have the belief system that his teacher doesn't like him. Your son's teacher may be able to lend insight into something that can be as minor as he is mad because he can't have his way within the class. His remedy is to "tell on the teacher" and let you know that it's their fault, or he could be very accurate about the teacher not liking him for reasons they don't even understand.

While working in central services, I had the distinct pleasure of being able to monitor both students and teachers. Often the monitoring of the teachers was at the discretion of the principal, and the teacher thought it was the student being observed, but sometimes it was them. Several major themes often occurred as I was observing the dynamics of the teacher/student relationship.

Teachers did not know anything about their students after the school day was over

(For example: did they play a sport; did they have a pet or a baby sister or brother at home)? This lack of personal knowledge was very prevalent with Caucasian female teachers and African American male students.

Teachers had different expectations for different students

(For example I had a high school guidance counselor tell me that she did not encourage her African American students to attend Duke University because she did not want to set them up for failure. I remember the entire table (we were at a luncheon) became quiet to allow her to finish the ridiculous statement that she had begun. After a lot of "back peddling", she finally left the table in tears because she had exposed herself as a racist and she knew now that her secret was out).

Some teachers had the Savior Syndrome

Caucasian female teachers often wanted to work with "inner-city" youth because they come out of college with the "savior syndrome." They want to "save" the students from their miserable existence by trying to get them out, yet become frustrated because that's not the purpose of teaching.

The world is based on white middle-class America

Some teachers are not culturally competent to work with all students, nor do they try to obtain competence in order for the students to become successful in public school.

White privilege is the "Elephant in the Room"

White privilege is unearned social, political, economic, and societal privileges that non-White persons don't have. White privilege is neither identified, acknowledged or attempted to be rectified by White America as it pertains to public education. No one wants to have courageous conversations about race; however, race is the reason that there is a gap in education. The reality of white privilege is important to discuss because more than 80% of teachers are Caucasian or white.

So you see, parent, it could be that your son's teacher doesn't like him and she/he doesn't even know why. The task for you is to find out if this is true and if it is true, then why.

Questions to Ask Your Son's Teacher

1) What do you know about my son? What are his likes, dislikes, his distinguishing positive and negative characteristics? For every one negative thing the teacher has to say (i.e. talks too much), he/she should be able to say two nice things as well.

2) What do you know about my son's family?

3) Does my son, based on your observation, like school? In your opinion, why or why not?

4) What makes you culturally competent to teach my child? (A culturally competent teacher is one who can effectively teach students within cross-cultural situations, who have an ethnicity and a culture that is unlike their own. Having African-American friends or a relative does not count).

5) Would you be willing to sit down with my son and me to talk with us about your class, your expectations as his teacher, your expectations of him as a learner, and how you will aid him in his learning process?

Dear Parent, if this does not work, or you do not feel as though your son's teacher will ever like him or if the relationship could never be repaired, then it is time to move him to a classroom environment where he can receive the love, acceptance, and nurturing that he needs to be a success. Remember, we are not moving a child based on your likes and dislikes, but based upon genuine, honest assessment, as a last resort when all other options are exhausted.

Parent's Tip: Your son's teacher may not like him! It is your responsibility as a parent to find a culturally competent teacher who does and who loves other people's children.

5

"You Are the Lead Teacher!"

"Children are like wet cement. Whatever falls on them makes an impression."
Author Unknown

Parents, your son will take his lead from you! You are his first teacher; mom you are the first woman that he will ever love and dad, you are the first man that he will ever respect. His impressions of who you are as people are an important part of what shapes him as a man.

The younger he is, the more impressionable he becomes. Pre-K through third grade are his most formidable (capable of learning) years.

Be careful that he does not take your hang-ups, misguided notions of race, education, and how to get along with people who do not look like him, to school.

The day is inevitable he will encounter race. Not only race, but racism, and he will have to make decisions. Make sure all of the decisions he must make as a man are informed decisions. Information based on fact, not fiction, nor opinion. Information based on love, not hate, and based upon tolerance, nothing that is fake.

Teach your son early, who he is, whose he is, and what his destiny and purpose are upon the earth. Identify his strengths, so that he can withstand anything and his weaknesses so he is aware of the areas where he will be tested the most.

Remind him of who he is REALLY; of where he REALLY comes from and of what is paramount in this life.

As you are parenting him, don't major in minors and minor in majors. In other words, don't overemphasize what is least important over what is important. For example, behavior IS important, but so is growth and growth potential. Behavior is not always an indicator that a child can't learn, often it is a symptom of other issues. Finding out the issue is important.

Don't over emphasize fluff and under emphasize importance.

Mom, model the woman, you want him to marry. Dad, model the man, that you would desire for him to become.

Encourage him to take school seriously, but not as serious as his learning; which comes in all forms, shapes, sizes, colors, and from all people in various capacities.

Allow him to play hard, but only after he works hard, within the classroom, and within your home.

Teach him how to value what he has so he can keep what he will own.

> **Parent's Tip:** Don't ever devalue the importance of you as his teacher!

6

"What Now?"

"There is another way to approach reform, a way that includes collaboration with the teachers, instead of bullying them or insulting them. A way that involves the community rather than imposing top-down decisions."
Zuckerberg's Expensive Lesson
NY Times

Get involved in your son's school! You may not like or appreciate all things "public education", but unless you are going to enroll in a charter or a private school or perhaps homeschool him, you need to get informed and get involved!

Don't ever approach the school in a hostile way. They will label you as they have your son, and you will get nothing accomplished.

Get to know your son's teacher. Not from the position of wanting to "get him/her told", but from the position of establishing the village to raise your son. You can't use the excuse, "I can't go to the school because of work or when you get home", "I am too tired to go to PTA/PTO." I encourage you to take the day off, eat lunch with your son. Go on the field trip and be a chaperone. Volunteer to send in baked goods for the party or get extra school supplies for a student who is in need.

Get to know the parents of your son's friends. Don't allow him to go anywhere without you having first checked it out to make sure that it is okay and safe. At the age of Pre-K to 3rd grade, they are still in need of a chaperone when going to parties, games, or church functions. Don't ever assume that someone loves or cares about your child as much as you do.

Don't ever approach the school in a hostile way. They will label you as they have your son, and you will get nothing accomplished.

Remember This

Interview the school/learning center in Pre-K.

Ensure the philosophy of the learning institution is the same as your philosophy of learning and education. Make sure religious beliefs and practices are congruent with yours, and the staff is qualified to perform their assigned duties.

Interview your child's teacher before the beginning of the academic school year.

Take a tour of the school with your son to gain discernment and to see if this is the type of school that will be conducive to a productive learning environment. Hint: Every organization is only as good as the head. Make sure you meet the Principal and talk about his/her philosophy of education and learning. Ask about his/her leadership style. You will know if this is accurate based upon the teacher's response to the same question. It should be congruent. If the teacher seems disgruntled with the principal or the principal with the teacher, then be aware that there may be signs of impending issues.

Assess the atmosphere of the school.

Is the staff happy, joyous, look eager to be there? Or do they whisper and roll their eyes at the building administrator behind his/her back?

Discuss expectations as family.

Talk to your son, along with your spouse, about expectations within the home, as a student, as a learner, and as a son. Encourage him by giving him the learning styles and multiple intelligences test to find out the best way to facilitate his learning experience.

Explore other resources.

Scour the internet, Pinterest, or bookstores to find supplementary materials to work on with your son to further facilitate his learning experience.

Establish a routine and stick with it for the remainder of the academic school year.

Set a bedtime, set a time for playing/watching T.V.; outline specific chore duties, and give your son some responsibility in choosing his clothes in the morning. Allow him to groom himself, as well purchase him an alarm clock to make him responsible for getting up in the morning for school.

Maintain a balance between school, church, and community activities.

Too much of any of those is not good for your son. But a mixture of them makes him very well rounded and adaptable (colleges look for these types of students). Set the expectation, early, of being a scholar athlete and remind your son that playing sports or participating in any extracurricular activities such as band or Boy Scouts is a privilege, not a right.

Take charge of your son's learning experiences, as well as his discipline choices

Don't allow special education to come into play unless it is truly necessary. Make sure you have exhausted all responses to intervention, according to your local school district's policies. Special education plans should be utilized for academics, not behavior.

> **Parent's Tip:** Learning is power! Set the tone for your son to become a lifelong learner and to love it.

Final Thoughts

I believe being a parent is the most important assignment we will ever have in life, and you only have one chance to make a lasting impression. Your son's manhood is dependent upon his ability to navigate through the formative years of his life and you, parent, are an integral part of his shaping and developing. Let me encourage you, fellow parent, there is nothing more precious, upon this earth than the child that you have been entrusted with. Guard him, lead him, challenge him, encourage him, build him, and then allow him to be the man he was intended to be. Don't allow him to get crushed by public school. Work together, form partnerships, foster collaborations, build communities, and change a nation. Your son is depending on you!

About the Author

 Miranda Y. Pearson, LPCS, NCC, BCC, LCAS-A is a licensed public school teacher, supervising counselor, curriculum specialist, administrator, and ordained minister. Having been in public education since 1996, Miranda has taught English, served as a high school counselor, an Assistant Principal Intern, a District At-Risk Administrator and is currently serving, as Executive Director of NuFocus Enrichment Center, Inc. as well as Pastor of Selah Empowerment Ministries, Inc. She is also the owner and clinical director of Divine Appointment Counseling Service, PA.

She earned her B.S. in English from Radford University, in Radford, VA; MA in Christian Counseling from Andersonville Baptist Seminary, in Camilla, GA; MSA in School Administration, and an MS in Counselor Education, both from East Carolina University, in Greenville, NC. She is currently a doctoral learner in the field of Human Services, at Capella University, with a specialization in Counseling Studies; a doctoral student in Ministry at Andersonville Baptist Seminary, as well having completed a specialized certification in Substance Abuse Counseling/Contemporary Theory of Addictive Behavior.

Miranda is currently receiving Supervision to become a Licensed Clinical Addictions Specialist.

In addition to having a passion for teaching and counseling, Miranda loves to empower women in knowing their purpose and assisting them with their Kingdom assignments.

She enjoys spending quality time with her husband, Robert, as well as watching her son, Joshua, play and excel at basketball, football, and baseball.

Contact Miranda

If you are looking for a dynamic speaker, educator, and counselor, book Miranda Y. Pearson, Licensed Professional Counselor, National Certified Counselor, Board Certified Coach, Licensed Clinical Addictions Specialist Associate, for all of your educational, spiritual, and counseling needs. She will speak to your civic organizations, PTA/PTO organizations, community centers, churches, and educational conferences.

For booking, you can contact her at P.O. Box 1108, Benson, NC 27504, divineapptcounseling@yahoo.com, www.divineapptcounseling.com or 919-464-4255.

Made in the USA
Las Vegas, NV
12 February 2022